taking out the Tigers

Poems by Brian Moses

Illustrated by
Chris Garbutt

MACMILLAN CHILDREN'S BOOKS

To my daughter Karen – For a Dancer

First published 2005 by Macmillan Children's Books
a division of Macmillan Publishers Limited
20 New Wharf Road, London N1 9RR
Basingstoke and Oxford
www.panmacmillan.com

Associated companies throughout the world

ISBN: 978-0-330-41797-6

3 5 7 9 8 6 4

A CIP catalogue record for this book is available from
the British Library.

Printed and bound in Great Britain by Mackays of Chatham plc, Kent

Contents

The I-Spy Book of Teachers

One point if you catch your teacher yawning.
Double that to two if later on you find her snoring.
Three points if you hear your teacher singing
and four if it's a pop song not a hymn.
A generous five points if you ever see them jogging
and six if you should chance upon them snogging.
Seven if you ever find her on her knees and praying
for relief from noisy boys who trouble her.
Eight if you should catch him in the betting shop,
nine if you see him dancing on *Top of the Pops*.
And ten if you hear her say what a lovely class she's got
for then you'll know there's something
   quite seriously wrong with her.

Tasting the Sea

Apparently
there were Cornish sea captains
who could tell exactly where they were
when mist and lack of lights conspired
to hide the coast from view.
When a storm had locked them
on a course for rocks
they could tell the shore
they were heading towards
by tasting the sea.

And these old soaks,
these old sea rovers,
would command the first mate
to hang overboard
and scoop up a cup of sea.
Then holding it up to the light
they'd argue over the colour.
They'd sniff, take a sip,
then swirl it about in the mouth
before spitting it out,
till one of their number,
with further thought would announce:

Too bitter for Lizard,
too salty for Sennen,
too clean for Pendeen,
too clear for Porthmear

It's here we are, he'd say
with certainty, jabbing a finger
down on the chart.

Then heads would nod
and an order be given
to turn the ship for home,
with a ration of rum for everyone
to celebrate
their escape.

The Song

I came to Dublin to look for the song,
for some wayward melody
that, once heard, would be remembered,
but the song discovered me.

It was a message from a busker
in the hustle of Grafton Street,
I caught it escaping from doorways,
picked it up in the rhythm of feet,

I heard it splash in the Liffey,
I heard its blah! blah! blahs!
Every night it was telling wild stories
in a hundred smoky bars.

I heard it midnight drunk
till it sounded like a threat,
a bruised and broken version,
one that I'd rather forget.

I pursued it over a bridge
and up the Winding Stair,
then lost it in Quayside traffic
but couldn't abandon it there.

I caught it again in a saxophone
blowing such an aching tune,
I heard African drumbeats lift it up
and bounce it off the moon.

It hid from me on O'Connell Street,
became part of the evening crowd,
then revealed itself in Temple Bar,
bold and brash and loud.

And I know it can never be captured,
it demands its freedom to roam,
but I'm hoping still that a part of the song
will follow me back home.

Dublin, April 2002

How Teachers Leave School Each Evening

The dance teacher floats down the stairway
and waltzes herself to the door.
Behind her the maths teacher counts every step
as he paces across the floor.

The geography teacher struggles to find
a different route home each night.
The PE teacher sets new daily records
for the swiftest homeward flight.

The English teacher recites to himself
lines of poetry by Keats.
The drama teacher's on camera,
a movie star in the streets.

The RE teacher prays
that there'll be no traffic queues.
The physics teacher knows there will
and regularly blows a fuse.

The IT teacher imagines he's left
as he follows some virtual route on screen.
It's a mystery why the history teacher
is met each night by a limousine.

Our music teacher, an Elvis freak,
plays air guitar along the drive.
With his rocker's quiff and Las Vegas suit
he's out there somewhere perfecting his jive.

But the teacher who's young and still keen
reluctantly closes the door,
ticks off the hours and minutes till she can be
back with her class once more.

Incident in New York City

The Department of Superheroes
heard a desperate telephone plea.
'Bring needle and thread,' a voice demanded,
'and bring them straight here to me.'

Then the voice explained what had happened
and how circumstances were dire:
Superman had just torn his tights
on the Empire State Building's spire.

Playing with Stars

Young children know what it's like
to play with stars.

First of all it's a wink and a smile
from some distant constellation,
then it's hide and seek as they disappear
in a cover of cloud.
Sometimes children see how far
they can travel to a star
before familiar voices call them
home to bed.

Like all good games, of course,
you need to use a little imagination
when playing with stars.
More experienced players
can jump over stars
or shake down a star.
Some can trap them in butterfly nets,
but you should always let them loose again.
Stars grow pale and die if you cage them.

Sometimes the stars tell stories
of their journeys across the sky
and sometimes they stay silent.
At these times children may travel themselves,
wandering a line that unravels
through their dreams.
At these times too, the stars play their own games,
falling from the sky when there's no one there
to catch them.

Sometimes you find these stars on the ground,
dazed and confused. Be warned though,
even fallen stars may be hot to touch.

Young children know what it's like
to rescue stars, to hold them gently
in gloved hands and then,
with one almighty fling,
sling them back to the sky.

Adults forget what it's like
to play with stars
and when children offer to teach them,
they're far too busy.

A Feather from an Angel

Anton's box of treasures held
a silver key and a glassy stone,
a figurine made of polished bone
and a feather from an angel.

The figurine was from Borneo,
the stone from France or Italy,
the silver key was a mystery
but the feather came from an angel.

We might have believed him if he'd said
the feather fell from a bleached white crow
but he always replied, 'It's an angel's, I know,
a feather from an angel.'

We might have believed him if he'd said,
'An albatross let the feather fall.'
But he had no doubt, no doubt at all,
his feather came from an angel.

'I thought I'd dreamt him one night,' he'd say,
'but in the morning I knew he'd been there;
he left a feather on my bedside chair,
a feather from an angel.'

And it seems that all my life I've looked
for that sort of belief that nothing could shift,
something simple yet precious as Anton's gift,
a feather from an angel.

Dear Yuri

Dear Yuri, I remember you,
the man with the funny name
who the Russians sent into space,
were you desperate for fame?

There surely must have been safer ways
to get into the history books,
perhaps you couldn't rock like Elvis
or you hadn't got James Dean's looks.

Perhaps you couldn't fight like Ali
or make a political speech
so they packed you into a spaceship
and sent you out of Earth's reach.

And, Yuri, what was it like
to be way out there in space,
the first to break free of Earth's gravity
and look down on the human race?

I'd been doing my maths all morning
and at lunchtime I heard what you'd done.
I told everyone back at school
how you'd rocketed near to the sun.

And, Yuri, I wanted to say
that I remember your flight,
I remember your name, Gagarin,
and the newsreel pictures that night.

And you must have pep talked others
when they took off into the blue.
I've forgotten their names, but, Yuri,
I'll always remember you.

The Children of Witches

*In the witchcraft trials of the early seventeenth century,
the evidence of children was considered acceptable.
Judges were keen to make as many convictions
as they could in order to please King James I, who
considered himself an expert on the matter.*

Mark is the son of a blacksmith,
John's folk keep pigs and dig ditches,
but Robert and Jessie and me,
we are the children of witches.

Mark is an expert at hunting,
John wins at games of chance,
but Robert and Jessie and me,
we saw the witches dance.

Mark is as tough as an anvil,
John has wings on his feet,
but Robert and Jessie and me,
we know where the witches meet.

Mark sings aloud in the choir,
John prays at home every day,
but Robert and Jessie and me,
we gave the witches away.

We were easily tricked by questions,
was it truth we should tell or a lie?
So we told tales on the witches
and condemned our mothers to die.

Soon Mark will start work in the smithy
while John helps his father dig ditches.
But there's no certain future for any of those
who are tainted as children of witches.

America's Gate
(Ellis Island)

'I'm bringing something beautiful to America.'
(Girl, 10 years)

If I miss my name
   then I might be forever knocking
      on America's gate.
If I lose my ticket and miss my turn
   I may never learn the lie of this land.
For all that I've planned
   is tied up in this trip,
all that I own
   is packed up in this bag.
And there isn't much money
   but there's gifts I can bring.
And I'm bringing them all to America,
I'm bringing them all from home.
Not my mother's rings
   or my party dress,
not my father's watch
   or my lacy shawl,
just the moon on my shoulder,
   a voice that can sing,
feet that can dance

and a pipe that I play.
And I'm playing now for America,
    and I'm hoping that someone will notice.
Then perhaps I won't be here forever
knocking on America's gate.

The School Goalie's Reasons Why Each Goal Shouldn't Have Been a Goal in a Match That Ended 14:0 to the Visiting Team

1. It wasn't fair, I wasn't ready . . .
2. Their striker was offside, it was obvious . . .
3. Phil got in my way, he always gets in my way, he should be dropped . . .
4. I had something in my eye . . .
5. I hadn't recovered from the last one that went in, or the one before that . . .
6. I thought I heard our head teacher calling my name . . .
7. Somebody exploded a blown-up crisp bag behind me . . .
8. There was a beetle on the pitch, I didn't want to tread on it . . .
9. Somebody exploded another blown-up crisp bag . . .
10. That girl in Year 5 was smiling at me, I don't like her doing that . . .
11. The goalposts must have been shifted, they weren't as wide before . . .
12. I thought I saw a UFO fly over the school . . .
13. There was a dead ringer for David Beckham watching us, he was spooky . . .

And goal number 14?

It just wasn't a goal, I'm sorry, it just wasn't a goal and that's that.

OK?

River Don

How fortunate is Don
to have a river named after him.
I wish I had something
named after me.
River Brian doesn't sound quite right,
nor does Brian Street or Brian Road.
(There was a Brian Close once,
but he was a cricketer.)
Scotland does interesting things with names.
I'd love to be the Pass of Brian
or the Bridge of Brian – that sounds good.
The name Brian means strength,
tough as cowhide, strong as iron;
maybe I could be the Mountain of Brian.
If I wanted it to reflect the very core of me,
the very heart, if I wanted it to conjure up
the very Brianness of Brian,
I'd find the River Brian flowing in my veins,
Fortress Brian in the heart of me,
Church of Brian in my soul.
And in my eyes, the Great Fire of Brian,
to be glimpsed by everyone
and admired!

Zoo of Winds

Wild winds have escaped tonight,
and like animals suddenly loose from a zoo
they are out doing damage.
We hear them snaking
into cracks and crevices
while beasts
with the strength of buffaloes
batter the building.
Shrill birds whistle through the hallway
and a lion's roar seems stuck
in the chimney.
A howling hyena is caught
in the porch
while a horrid hook of a claw
tries to splinter the loft hatch.
All manner of fearsome creatures
lunge down the lane
while our garden is buffeted
by the angry breath of bears.
I hope someone soon
recaptures these beasts,
locks them away,
cages them tightly.
These winds are not welcome visitors,
not tonight, not any time.

Moon over Madrid

There's a moon over Madrid tonight,
a bright, inquisitive moon
that's about as full as it gets.
For me, it's something familiar
in an unfamiliar city,
a reference point on these Spanish streets.
It keeps me company, sometimes slipping
out of sight, dodging behind buildings
then reappearing, while I'm thinking
how the moon holds a thread
that ties us together.
'Look up at the moon,' I tell you.
'Look at the moon and imagine that thread
as a line linking you
to the mountains of the moon
and then down to the streets of Madrid.
That same moon touching your life,
now touches mine too.'

The Never-Stop-Moving Family

The never-stop-moving family
is ruining our holiday,
making us feel really guilty,
we wish that they'd go away.
They're outside before breakfast
doing fifty press-ups each,
then kitted out they're jogging off
for tennis on the beach.
Then it's back for another workout
before jumping on their bikes
or strapping on their rucksacks
and starting ten-mile hikes.
Then it's down to the beach again
with their wetsuits and their boards
and a final session at the gym
just leaves us lost for words.
They must have wings on their ankles
or flames that lick their feet.
Something keeps them powered up,
maybe it's something they eat!

We suspect they've labelled us
the lazy family,
no energy or enthusiasm
for sporting activity.
But we're not here to race about,
face challenges or march up a hill,
we're here for one reason only,
we're simply here to chill!

Kirk Deighton

Kirk Deighton?
That can't be the name of a place!
Sounds more like the name
of a superhero, a '00' agent,
someone to swoon over.
Kirk Deighton,
suave, sophisticated,
a gold-plated gun in a
shoulder holster,
hairy chest, bullet-proof
vest.
The kind of guy that
girls adore,
a secret spy on a
dangerous mission
somewhere off the
A1, South
Yorkshire.

Wish

Clasp in your hand
the single black feather
left in your garden
as a gift from a crow.

Whisper the words
that you learned from the wind,

Find dragonfly spit
and a snake's shed skin.

Find a flower's heartbeat
and the moon's lost silver,

Now gather them together
with the crow's black feather . . .

and WISH . . .

The Celtic Cat

(I don't know if there is any connection between cats and dragons in Celtic mythology, I suspect not. But it would be interesting if there was.)

The Celtic Cat is familiar with dragons,
It knows their secrets, has visited their lairs.
It has admired itself in the mirrored shields
of dragons' treasure troves.
It has singed its tail and whiskers
in the heat of their fire.

The Celtic cat travels to the places
where dragons gather. It would willingly
surrender the lives it has
for an offer of eternity.
And yet there is already much of the dragon
in the cat itself – a hologram of flame
in its eyes, claws that could rip a hole
in the fabric of our world, through which
myths and memories pour out.

The Celtic cat understands that once,
dragons knew everything —
it desires that knowledge for itself . . .
A dragon's tongue, a dragon's teeth, a dragon's heart,
soon they will belong to the Celtic cat,
and the cherished secret of flight revealed
from the deepest wells of a dragon's soul.
For this is its birthright, its destiny,
cat and dragon, one and the same,
eyes, wings, dragon flame . . .

St David's, 2003

The Theme for This Week Is 'Laziness'

(From a sign in the hall at Godshill School, Isle of Wight!)

I've never been very good at school,
it's not often that I do well,
but the theme for this week is 'laziness'
and that's something at which I excel.

I have no trouble being lazy,
it's really no effort at all.
I prefer to watch television
than be outside chasing a ball.

I'm always last to finish my work,
I always come last in a race.
I never get any group points,
my teacher says I'm a disgrace.

But everyone's good at something
and at laziness I'll be the best.
I know that I'm good at laziness
and I'll happily take any test.

Perhaps next week we'll do 'carelessness',
there's 'clumsiness' and 'thoughtlessness' too.
I'm good at all these, but I'm just no good
at subjects they want me to do.

I'm a lazy good-for-nothing,
that's something I've always been told,
but if laziness were an Olympic sport
then I know I'd be going for gold!

The Weirdest Exhibit

The museum galleries
go on for miles,
you see furniture and furnishings,
tapestries and tiles.
You see kitchens where fire grates
are blackened with soot,
but the weirdest exhibit
is a mummified foot.

It's gruesome and gross
but you'll love it the most,
the Egyptian mummified foot.

You can see right inside
where the skin has been ripped,
then you'll notice the bone
and the way it's been chipped.
And beneath the bandage
you'll see actual flesh . . .
I bet it smelt cheesy
even when it was fresh!

It's gruesome and gross
but you'll love it the most,
the Egyptian mummified foot.

And what's so amazing,
what's really fantastic,
the toenails are real
and not made of plastic.
And beneath the nails
you can see grains of sand.
Are they picked at each night
by a mummified hand?

It's gruesome and gross
but you'll love it the most,
the Egyptian mummified foot.

Visiting Jupiter

There must be some celestial M25
all the way to Jupiter,
or how else can you explain
why it takes six years to get there?
Six years without a service station on the way.
Six years of stopping and starting
and travelling through roadworks,
single carriageway all the way to Venus.
And what would it be like for any spaceman
travelling there?
'Just slipping out to visit Jupiter,
see you soon, don't wait up . . .'
Not much scope for holidays either,
no possibilities of day trips or weekend breaks.
Six years!
What are you doing for the next six years?
Think of all the books you could read,
the games you could play – not I-spy though.
'I-spy with my little eye something beginning
with S . . . Yes, SPACE,
lots of it,
how did you guess?'

Hang-gliding over Active Volcanoes

It was truly amazing the first time I dared,
like surfin' in a furnace, but wow, was I scared!
That first time I tried it, I nearly died,
grilled to perfection on the underside.

Yes, I got singed from my eyebrows to my toes
from hang-gliding over active volcanoes.

I saw bubbling lava, fountains of fire,
felt warm blasts lifting me even higher.
I was floating along on waves of steam
while applying layers of suntan cream.

Yes, I got singed from my eyebrows to my toes
from hang-gliding over active volcanoes.

And it didn't take long to get me really hooked
on that great sensation of feeling half cooked.
What a thrill, I could chill in this situation
if I don't succumb to asphyxiation.

Yes, I got singed from my eyebrows to my toes,
I got scorched from my kneecaps to my nose
from hang-gliding over active volcanoes.

Taking Out the Tigers

At twilight time
or early morning
a tiger-sized ROAR
is a fearsome warning
as a huge cat swaggers
through a fine sea mist,
its paws the size
of a boxer's fist,

when they're
taking out the tigers
on Sandown beach.

These tough kitties
have something to teach
about the law of the jungle
on Sandown beach.
And any kind of dog
would be most unwise
to challenge a cat
that's this sort of size,

when they're
taking out the tigers
on Sandown beach.

As a weak sun sinks
in a winter sky,
it reflects in the jewel
of a tiger's eye,
but an Indian Ocean
is dreams away
from the chilly surf
of Sandown Bay,

when they're
taking out the tigers
on Sandown beach,
taking out the tigers
on Sandown beach,
taking out the tigers . . .

Our Ditch

I sat and thought one day
of all the things we'd done
with our ditch; how we'd jumped across
at its tightest point, till I slipped
and fell, came out smelling,
then laid a pole from side to side,
dared each other to slide along it.
We fetched out things that others threw in,
lobbed bricks at tins, played Pooh-sticks.
We buried stuff in the mud and the gunge
then threatened two girls with a ducking.
We floated boats and bombed them,
tiptoed along when the water was ice,
till something began to crack, and we scuttled back.
We borrowed Mum's sieve from the baking drawer,
scooped out tadpoles into a jar
then simply forgot to put them back.
(We buried them next to the cat.)

Then one slow day in summer heat
we followed our ditch to where it began,
till ditch became stream, and stream
fed river, and river sloped off to the sea.
Strange, we thought, our scrap of water
growing up and leaving home,
roaming the world and lapping
at distant lands.

Three Mammoth Poems

1. Why?

Why was a mammoth called a mammoth
and not an 'enormous' or a 'colossal'?
And how did they know what to call it
when they first discovered a fossil.

2. Mammoth Toothache

I wonder if mammoth dentists
were skilled in pulling mammoth teeth.
What a mammoth task it must have been
to pull from above and push from beneath.

And it must have been terribly painful
without any anaesthetic,
but if anyone let slip a mammoth scream
they'd be labelled a wimp or pathetic.

So mammoths put up with toothache
instead of admitting their molars were sore.
They wore a pained expression, till the ache
was just something they couldn't ignore.

Then trembling they'd visit the dentist
and tell him to kill the pain
and the tooth would be pulled, then dropped
in the ice that covered some mammoth plain.

So be grateful that you're not a mammoth
with a carpet like cover of wool
and be grateful too that your teeth are tiny
and fairly painless to pull.

3. Fossil
Now many years from the Ice Age
a fossilized piece of bone
helps us make sense of the mammoth
like an ancient text message in stone.

Lost Kitty in New York City ($500 Reward)

Nothing has been heard,
not a single word
about the lost kitty
in New York City.
No word from the birds,
it's quite absurd.
The rats won't rat,
the mice said, 'Scat,
it's rat-a-tat-tat
if we find that cat.'

On Madison Square
she was nowhere.
Up the Empire State
it was too late.

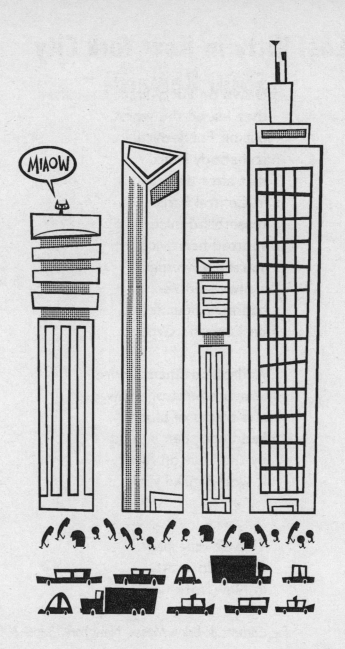

Down on Forty-first
they feared the worst,
but on Forty-third
somebody heard
that after dark
in Central Park,
three blind mice
spotted her twice,
started a whisper,
a silver whisker
had now been found
on Lennon's Ground.

And one of them swore
that the print of a paw
and tracks of blood
had been seen in mud
by the Hudson River —
it would make you
                    shiver . . .

There's little pity
for any lost kitty
in New York City.

Pie Corbett & Brian Moses, New York, Sept. 2000

46

lonelydinosaur.com

lonelydinosaur.com
has just appeared on the World Wide Web.
And up till now there's never been
a place for those who escaped extinction
to meet and date and possibly mate.
But now there's a dating agency
with all sorts of dinosaurs on its books,
where looks are unimportant
and what really matters is personality,
how much charm one creature
can offer another.

So dinosaurs, wherever you're hiding,
turn on to the new technology,
let them match your details
with dinosaurs on their database.
And before you know it
you'll be out on a date, well on the way
to finding a mate. So take a look
at what's on offer . . .

T. Rex would like to meet T. Rex
for friendship or even romance.
Brontosaurus needs similar
for sociable wallowing.
Triceratops needs another
to shop till they drop,
while a lonely velociraptor
would welcome some fun with anyone.
But it isn't considered a good idea
for carnivores to date herbivores
as 'Nice to meet you' may quickly turn
into 'Very nice to *eat* you'.

But really this is the greatest chance
for dinosaurs to find romance,
for all the lost and lonely ones
who partied too hard
and stayed too long,
who have wandered the world's
most desolate places . . .
just get on the net
and find a mate,
call lonelydinosaur.com

High-Flyers

We thought our teacher was ordinary,
we thought she was really boring,
she always looked tired from teaching us
and at weekends was probably snoring.
We thought she led a quiet life
at home, feet up, being lazy,
but it seemed that our teacher had always wanted
to try something really crazy . . .

She told us all in the middle of maths
she'd be doing a bungee jump,
and we were appalled, we could see her
hitting the ground with a mighty thump.
We were worried it wouldn't be anything else
but one hundred per cent disaster,
our teacher laid out in a hospital bed
with both of her legs in plaster.

She'd be raising lots of money, she said,
for her favourite charity,
but we felt it would be far too much
for a woman of fifty-three.
Then she said, I hope you'll support me,
I expect you all to be there.
It's Saturday afternoon at three,
halfway through our village fair.

So we all turned up and had to admit
our teacher looked fantastic,
and we watched amazed as she bounced around
on the end of a length of elastic.
She was kitted out in a jumpsuit
that was zigzag yellow and black
and reminded us all of an angry wasp
that was moving in to attack.

But that wasn't the only surprise of the day
because tumbling down from the sky
was a team of free-fall divers
who we couldn't identify,
till their parachutes suddenly blossomed
and somebody started to laugh,
when drifting gently down to earth
came the rest of our school staff!

Giant's-eye View
(From the Grossmünster Tower, Zurich)

It's great to get a giant's-eye view
of this city,
to see what a bird sees every day,
to be in a world of steeples and towers,
people down below not knowing
they're watched . . .

I'd like to reach down
and rearrange the streets.
Like a mischievous giant with elastic arms
I could derail trams, cause traffic jams,
move parked cars to different spaces,
wipe the smile from people's faces
by flipping them into the river
with my finger flicks . . .

With my giant's eye I could spy into skylights,
I could snoop in hidden courtyards.
I could block chimneys with my thumbs,
re-route smoke through the rooms below.

And all the birds thinking they're safe,
that the skyways belong to them.
Be gone, gulls, scram, pigeons,
there'll be no sky-walking on my rooftops.

For one trifling moment
I'd be the hidden boss of this city,
leave my giant's mark and feel the power
of the writer who scratched at the tower top:
Ich war hier . . .
I WAS HERE!

The Fear

I am the footsteps that crackle on gravel
and the sudden chill that's hard to explain.
I am the figure seen flitting through doorways
and the noisy rattle of a loose windowpane.

I am the scream that wakes you at night
with the thought, was it real or a dream?
I am the quickening thud of your heart
and the feeling things aren't what they seem.

I am the slam of a door blown shut
when there isn't even a breeze
and the total and absolute certainty
that you just heard someone sneeze.

I am the midnight visitor,
the knock when there's no one there.
I am the ceiling creaking
and the soft footfall on your stair.

I am the shadows that dance on your wall
and the phantoms that float through your head.
And I am the fear that you feel each night
as you wriggle down deep in your bed.

The ET Runway

It is rumoured that in the Nevada Desert in America there is a specially prepared ET Runway with welcome messages permanently beamed into the sky to attract the attention of low-flying extraterrestrials. Meanwhile, in a back garden in Sussex . . .

We've laid out what looks like a landing strip
in the hope of attracting an alien ship
and we've even managed to rig up a light
that will flash on and off throughout the night.
And we've spelt out 'welcome' in small white stones
and we've messed around with two mobile phones
till now they bleep almost continuously
and their signals play havoc with next-door's TV.
But it's for the greater good of mankind,
this could be a really important find.

And we're going to have an interstellar fun day
when aliens land on *our* ET runway.
What a day it will be and what a surprise
when alien spacecraft snowflake the skies,
when strange beings christen our welcoming mat
to gasps of amazement, 'Just look at that!'
And to anyone out there listening in
the reception we'll give you is genuine:

WELCOME

We promise there'll be no limousines
to take you to tea with kings and queens.
No boring politicians from different lands,
no chatting on chat shows, or shaking of hands,
no scientists waiting to whisk you off
to investigate every bleep, grunt or cough.
It will only be us, just me and Pete
and a few friends from school you'll be happy to meet.
We could interview you for the school magazine:
'Do your spacecraft run on gasoline?'

And we know it's not the desert in Nevada,
but we really couldn't have tried much harder.
So if you can hear us please make yourself known,
send us a signal, pick up the phone.
We've seen you out there, effortlessly gliding,
introduce yourselves now, it's time to stop hiding.

Classroom Globe

We strung our globe from the rafters
then watched how the continents spun.
We were dizzy with faraway places,
they swam before our eyes.
Everyone wanted to take a swipe at
the planet, to roll the world, to cause
global chaos. We laughed at the
notion of some great hand, sweeping down
avalanches, rolling earthquakes round
Africa, knocking elephants off their feet.
Then reasons were found for leaving seats,
to touch or tilt or hit heads on the planet,
squaring up to the world like March hares.
We talked of how the Earth had been damaged,
leaving it bruised, sore from neglect,
and Jenny, who feels sorry for anyone and
anything, leaned her brow against the planet
and felt the sorrow and pain of Earth
in a cold hard globe.

The American Bored Eagle

This is the American bored eagle
shackled to its perch like a criminal,
and nothing is as bored as a bored eagle
far from the pull of an American sky.

I wonder who took the first bald eagle
and tore its heart from the wilderness.
I wonder who manacled its spirit
and timetabled its flight.

And maybe now, on that one daily glide
in the exercise yard of an English sky,
something still turns this bored eagle's eye
to the swoop and dive of the slopes.

But the lure of the bait in the keeper's fist
means the drop from the sky is too easy,
the mountains now are too distant,
the memories too misty.

Cakes in the Staffroom

Nothing gets teachers more excited
than cakes in the staffroom at breaktime.
Nothing gets them more delighted
than the sight of plates
piled high with jammy doughnuts
or chocolate cake.

It's an absolute stampede
as the word gets round quickly,

And it's, 'Oooh these are really delicious,'
and, 'Aaah these doughnuts are great.'

And you hear them say, 'I really shouldn't,'
or, 'Just a tiny bit, I'm on a diet.'

Really, it's the only time they're quiet
when they're cramming cakes into their mouths,
when they're wearing a creamy moustache,
or the jam squirts out like blood,
or they're licking chocolate
from their fingers.

You can tell when they've been scoffing,
they get lazy in literacy,
sleepy in silent reading,
nonsensical in numeracy,
look guilty in assembly.

But nothing gets teachers more excited
than cakes in the staffroom at breaktime,
unless of course
it's wine in the staffroom at lunchtime!

This Moment of Magic
(On finding snow in the Alps in August)
For Oliver

I'd like to stay here forever
and never go back.
I'd like to stay in this clean
and perfect place
where there's no one to spoil
this moment of magic,
no one to rip a jagged hole
in the way I feel,
no one colouring my view
with unkind words or stupid remarks.
Here it is my voice, mine alone
that echoes back from these mountains.
Nothing that threatens,
no jibes, no taunts,
just me and these mountains,
safe, serene.
I'd like to stay here forever
and never go back.

And yet going back now
will be all the easier
for knowing this place,
this one perfect place
is here.

The Wizard's Cat

When the wizard cast
a spell on his cat,
he was tired, it backfired
and now this cat
is only half the creature
it used to be,
but half a cat
is still company,
still purrs, still warms
the wizard's seat,
still rubs round his legs
and gets under his feet.
But half a cat
is disconcerting
for other cats
when fighting or flirting.
it's doubly feared
this weird half-cat,
this half invisible
acrobat.

The wizard is worried,
he knows that he should
redo the spell
and make it good.
But what would be left
if this spell should fail?
How much of his cat,
maybe only a tail.
The wizard too
might be incomplete,
just a wizard's legs
and a wizard's feet.
So best not to meddle
with what's been done,
surely half a cat
is better than none.

Dog People

Some people are people people,
other people are dog people.

You can recognize them by the way they walk,
elegantly, like a neatly manicured poodle,
proudly, like a satisfied sheepdog,
spiritedly, like a playful spaniel.

You can recognize them by the way they look,
sorrowfully, like an out-of-sorts bloodhound,
belligerently, like a boisterous bulldog,
guiltily, like a bone-stealing mongrel.

You can recognize them by the way they talk,
yappily, like a privileged Pekinese,
howlingly, like a lovesick Dobermann,
moaningly, like a left-at-home Labrador.

You can recognize them by the way they look at you,
hungrily, like a lean Alsatian,
knowingly, like an aloof lapdog,
scarily, like a territorial terrier.

You can recognize them by what they talk about,
different sizes of dog basket,
where to buy the crunchiest biscuits,
the best places to take exercise.

Yes, some people are dog people
but I am not.
I am a rabbit person.
Let me hop across and tell you
all I know about carrots.

Christmas All Year

You've got to admire
anyone wacky enough to leave
their Christmas lights up all year!
But in our street
that's what they do.
In our street it's Christmas
any time of year.
Even in the hottest August heat
it's Christmas in our street,
a time-warp Christmas, a leftover Christmas,
an out-of-place, in-your-face
sort of Christmas.

In our street the sun never shines,
it's always in shade.
Santa Claus beams from a doorway,
reindeers race for the rooftops.
It's a street where snowmen never melt
and icicles never drip.
Maybe there's some crumb of comfort
for the sentimental or the heartsick,
knowing that Christmas doesn't go away,
knowing that here in our street
there's no January through to November,
for every day is Christmas Day,
every month December.

The Stuck-on-the-A1 Party

On a sunny afternoon near Barnsley
we're side by side by side
by side by side
in the biggest traffic jam
since I don't know when,
and the guy in the car next door
leans out and shouts:
'Let's have a stuck-on-the-A1 party!'

So we fetch the picnic baskets
and the bottles of pop.
We get really friendly
and play silly games,
like 'Guess when the traffic
will start up again'!

We play 'Postman's Knock'
and this huge French lorry driver kisses Mum
and looks as if he'd like to do it again
till Dad says, 'Watch it, chum!'

And a guy in a van selling novelty goods
hands out party hats, balloons
and those things that you blow
to make a rude noise.

And caterers, off to some wedding,
pass round the vol-au-vents and the chicken drumsticks.
'We'll never make it now,' they say.

We swap addresses with people
from the car in front,
'If you're ever up this way again,
look us up . . .'

And then when a shout comes
to say that we're moving on
everyone says what a great time they've had
and couldn't we do it again sometime?

And I'm thinking that maybe they'll really catch on,
these A1 parties – they're fun!

Old Black Dog

Did you ever see such an old black dog?

A laze about in the warm French sun dog.
A pat me if you like
    but you won't make me get up and run dog.
A once upon a time I'd play
    with a ball in the park dog.
A now I'm too tired and I can't be bothered to bark
    dog.

A cats don't worry me like they used to do dog,
    but if one of them invades my space
        I still might show them a thing or two dog.
A don't expect me to hear you when you call dog.
A leave me to dream and let me sprawl dog.

A scratch my tummy,
    look for me
where it's sunny

    dog.

Skunks

You don't know what it's like
to be reviled, to be hated
or slated like we are.
You don't know what it's like
to be the subject of such bad press.
When Noah took us on to the Ark
you should have heard the complaints.
All the other creatures moved away
to the other side of the boat
till it almost capsized,
and we were lucky to stay afloat.
Noah made us stay out on deck
after that little escapade.
But you carry on, avoid us,
shun us, run away,
steer clear, we are not
for the faint-hearted or those
with sensitive noses.
We are, as you might say,
an acquired smell –
eau de skunk – you could never
bottle and sell us.
We are unique, the bad eggs,
the rotten apples,
we stink bomb your senses.

You are not impressed with us,
we will never be your dinner guests.
Somewhere out there,
in the places where bad smells linger
we wait – an explosion of unpleasantness
no air-freshener can combat.

Pirate DJs

In the 1960s radio stations were set up illegally on ships in the North Sea and 'pirate DJs' broadcast continuous rock music to Britain.

Listen out now for the pirate DJs
as they sail on the airwaves every day
hear the rappiest, snappiest music they play
those pirate DJs.

It's the pirate DJs with their stock of treasure
oldies but goldies to give you pleasure
this isn't work, it's a lifetime of leisure
for pirate DJs.

Just check out the deck and the sounds that they blow
but they won't let you go till you've heard all the show
and they'll talk between tunes till you feel that you know
those pirate DJs.

And they're giving out all kinds of advice
from the evils of weevils to cooking with rice
and the best way to rid your body of lice
those pirate DJs.

Those pirate DJs most days feeling unwell
playing rock as they roll with the North Sea swell
they're magicians who'll have you under their spell
those pirate DJs.

And of course they're much braver than ever we think
they'd keep spinning discs if their ship should sink
till the waters rolled over them, black as ink
those pirate DJs.

Then down on the sea bed you'd still hear them play
rocking the rocks while the sounds ricochet
from Amsterdam to the Bay of Biscay
those wonderful, wonderful pirate DJs.

The Phantom Fiddler

(A ghostly apparition said to haunt
Threshfield School in the Dales)

There can't be an apparition
in our school.
We have rules to stop anyone
getting in.
We have keypads and an intercom
to keep children from harm.
Yet it seems that something
has invaded our building,
something that I heard last night
as I scooted down the street.
A screeching sound
like a fiddler playing,
laying down a curious tune
by the light of a magical moon.

And as I peered through the window
into the gloom of 3B's room,
I caught a glimpse of children,
or were they imps,
dancing round to the sounds
a fiddler played.
And I had to admit
that the music captured me.

And I danced to the fiddler's tune
by the light of a magical moon.

Sensible people would have scuttled by,
they wouldn't have lingered like I did.
They wouldn't have looked in the fiddler's eye
or followed when he crooked his finger.
And I had no choice but to stay with him
as I danced to the tune he played
and the imps came too
as we danced in the street
by the light of a magical moon.

But something must have broken the spell,
something must have woken me up.
And I saw the imps for what they were,
nasty, ghastly, horrid things
that chased me all the way to the well
where I leaped in the holy water.

And that's where I was found
later that night,
when lights blazed over the hill,
shivering down in Lady's Well,
still hearing that phantom fiddler's tune
by the light of a magical moon.

Graffiti Boy

I'm Rory, yeah, and since I was a boy
I've been writing my name everywhere I go,
it was Rory in the wet sand,
Rory in the snow.
Rory scuffed in gravel,
Rory scrawled on walls.
I chalked my name on pavements,
in schools and shopping malls.
I've been marking out my territory
and others had better beware:
these streets belong to Rory,
challenge me if you dare.

Rory tells my story,
it speaks my history.
Read my name and wonder
at this boy of mystery.

Now my story's moved up a notch
as I spray my name these days.
I'm the aerosol king of the junction
with my artistic displays.
And I love to travel about
noticing my name,
it gives me a heck of a buzz,
it gives me a taste of fame.

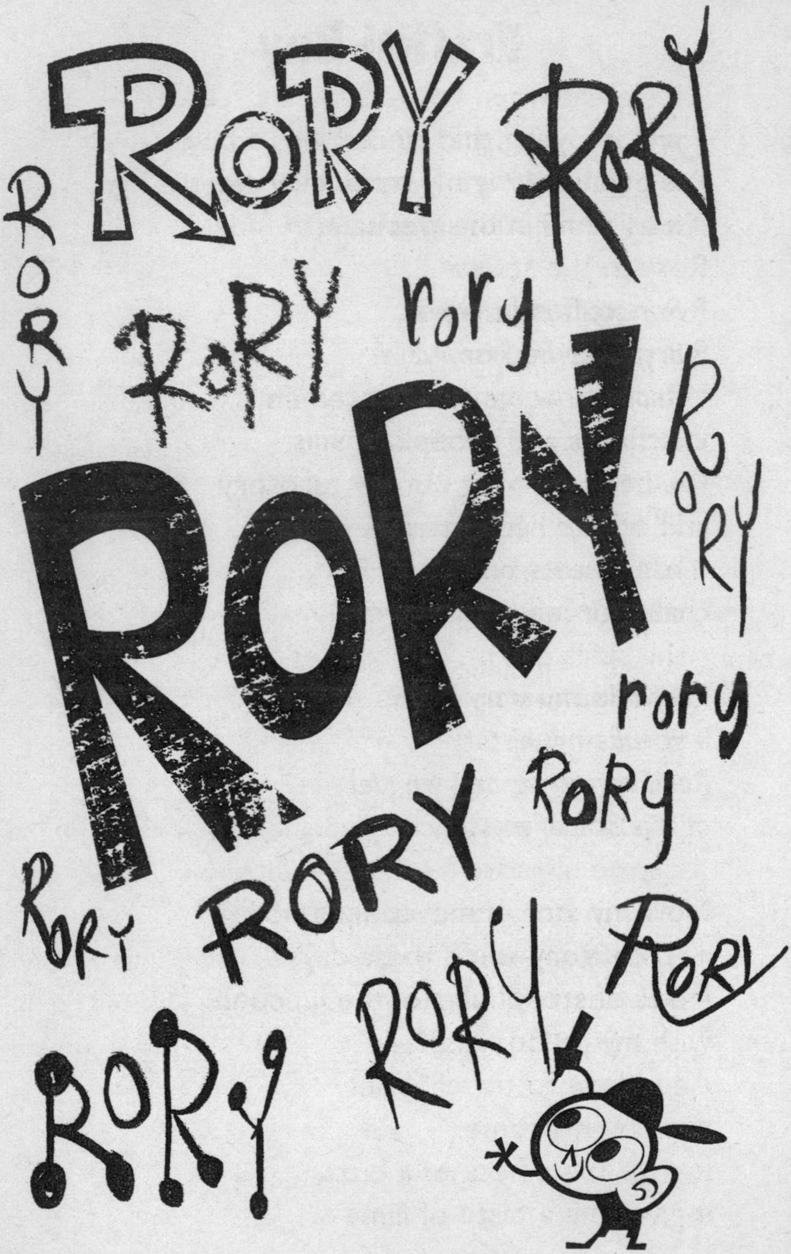

RORY
RORY
RORY
RORY
rory
RORY
RORY
rory
RORY
RORY
RORY
RORY
RORY
RORY

It's great when I'm walking a street
and knowing that round the next bend
is a place where I wrote my name,
it's like meeting up with a friend.

Rory tells my story,
it speaks my history.
Read my name and wonder
at this boy of mystery.

I'd like to see my name in lights,
I'd like to see it glow
and sometimes at night I imagine
the stars put on a show.
And looking up at the sky
you can guess at my elation,
my name across the heavens
in a brand-new constellation.
It's the ultimate piece of graffiti
that no one else could top.
I'd be Rory, universally,
end of story, full stop.

The Conker Season

Let's get down to the park and smash up a tree,
pull off branches and greenery,
it's the conker season again.

Don't consider the tree or the mess we leave,
throw sticks, throw bricks, give a mighty heave,
it's the conker season again.

Forget all those lessons we did at school
when being green was mega cool.
Don't care what we damage or break
when the conker championship's at stake.

Now the only prize is a heavyweight champ,
so pull down the fruit, smash and stamp,
it's the conker season again.

And till conker time's past, I know we'll be
environmentally *un*friendly,
it's the conker season again.

Billy's Coming Back

Word is out on the street tonight,
Billy's coming back.

There's a sound outside of running feet,
somebody, somewhere's switched on the heat,
policemen are beating a swift retreat
now Billy's coming back.

Only last year when he went away
everyone heaved a sigh,
now news is out, and the neighbourhood
is set to blow sky-high.

Words are heard in the staffroom,
teachers' faces deepen with gloom,
can't shrug off this feeling of doom
now Billy's coming back.

It was wonderful when he upped and left,
a carnival feeling straightaway,
no looking over shoulders,
each day was a holiday.

And now like a bomb no one dares to defuse,
time ticks on while kids quake in their shoes,
no winners here, you can only lose
now Billy's coming back.

It's dog eat dog on the street tonight,
it's cat and mouse, Billy's looking for a fight,
so take my advice, keep well out of sight
now Billy's coming back.

Postscript

Many of the poems in this book were inspired by visits to different places.

'America's Gate' and 'Lost Kitty in New York City' were both written in New York whilst on a visit there with my friend, the poet Pie Corbett. We spent a lot of time scribbling and 'Lost Kitty' was written together after we had seen a notice on Madison Avenue offering a reward of $500 for finding a lost cat.

When I visited Madrid I walked around a lot in the evening and a fat Spanish moon was the inspiration for 'Moon Over Madrid' – a poem about feeling a little bit lonely in a foreign city. It's dedicated to my friends at the Hastings School.

I love finding out strange facts about the different places that I visit and I owe the title poem, 'Taking Out the Tigers', to Roland Payn (Sham), deputy headteacher at Gurnard Primary School on the Isle of Wight. From Roland I learned about the tigers at Sandown Zoo and how they are sometimes exercised along the beach in winter.

Clare Griffiths, a teacher at Horndean Junior School in Hampshire, challenged me to write a poem about teachers and cakes. 'Cakes in the Staffroom' is for her and it seems to strike a familiar chord with many teachers!

School visits often give me ideas and 'The Theme For This week Is "Laziness"' came from a sign that I found in Godshill School, again on the Isle of Wight. Thanks to Jan for that!

'The Fear' was written whilst staying in a spooky castle on Guernsey, where I was working as resident writer.

'The Weirdest Exhibit' (a mummified foot) can actually be seen in the Cheltenham Museum.

Holidays are great times for writing. I always become an ideas detective seeking out inspiration from new experiences. A holiday in Pembrokeshire was particularly productive, resulting in 'If Houses Went on Holiday', 'The Celtic Cat' and 'The Never-Stop-Moving Family'. We were really shamed by the family next door to us — they must have been battery powered!

'Zoo of Winds' was the first poem I wrote after moving to a house in the country which has a long garden leading down to a field of cows. I hope that living in a different place, meeting new people and absorbing fresh experiences will give many more ideas for writing.

Until next time . . .

Brian Moses, June 2004

A selected list of poetry titles available from Macmillan Children's Books

The prices shown below are correct at the time of going to press. However, Macmillan Publishers reserves the right to show new retail prices on covers, which may differ from those previously advertised.

The Secret Lives of Teachers   978-0-330-43282-5   **£4.99**
Chosen by Brian Moses

The Works   978-0-330-48104-5   **£6.99**
Every kind of poem you will ever need for the Literacy Hour
Chosen by Paul Cookson

The Works 2   978-0-330-39902-9   **£6.99**
Poems on every subject and for every occasion
Chosen by Brian Moses and Pie Corbett

All Pan Macmillan titles can be ordered from our website,
www.panmacmillan.com, or from your local bookshop
and are also available by post from:

Bookpost, PO Box 29, Douglas, Isle of Man IM99 1BQ
Credit cards accepted. For details:
Telephone: 01624 677237
Fax: 01624 670923
Email: bookshop@enterprise.net
www.bookpost.co.uk

Free postage and packing in the United Kingdom